Department of Economic and Social Affairs

MW01517696

World Urbanization Prospects
The 2014 Revision

Highlights

United Nations
New York, 2014

Department of Economic and Social Affairs

The Department of Economic and Social Affairs of the United Nations Secretariat is a vital interface between global policies in the economic, social and environmental spheres and national action. The Department works in three main interlinked areas: (i) it compiles, generates and analyses a wide range of economic, social and environmental data and information on which States Members of the United Nations draw to review common problems and take stock of policy options; (ii) it facilitates the negotiations of Member States in many intergovernmental bodies on joint courses of action to address ongoing or emerging global challenges; and (iii) it advises interested Governments on the ways and means of translating policy frameworks developed in United Nations conferences and summits into programmes at the country level and, through technical assistance, helps build national capacities.

Note

The designations employed in this report and the material presented in it do not imply the expression of any opinion whatsoever on the part of the Secretariat of the United Nations concerning the legal status of any country, territory, city or area or of its authorities, or concerning the delimitation of its frontiers or boundaries.

Symbols of United Nations documents are composed of capital letters combined with figures.

Suggested citation:

United Nations, Department of Economic and Social Affairs, Population Division (2014). *World Urbanization Prospects: The 2014 Revision, Highlights (ST/ESA/SER.A/352).*

Cover photo: Asst. Prof. Chen Siyuan (2014) "Rocinha IV"

Published by the United Nations

Sales No. E.14.XIII.8

ISBN 978-92-1-151517-6

World Urbanization Trends 2014: Key Facts

- Globally, more people live in urban areas than in rural areas, with 54 per cent of the world's population residing in urban areas in 2014. In 1950, 30 per cent of the world's population was urban, and by 2050, 66 per cent of the world's population is projected to be urban.

- Today, the most urbanized regions include Northern America (82 per cent living in urban areas in 2014), Latin America and the Caribbean (80 per cent), and Europe (73 per cent). In contrast, Africa and Asia remain mostly rural, with 40 and 48 per cent of their respective populations living in urban areas. All regions are expected to urbanize further over the coming decades. Africa and Asia are urbanizing faster than the other regions and are projected to become 56 and 64 per cent urban, respectively, by 2050.

- The rural population of the world has grown slowly since 1950 and is expected to reach its peak in a few years. The global rural population is now close to 3.4 billion and is expected to decline to 3.2 billion by 2050. Africa and Asia are home to nearly 90 per cent of the world's rural population. India has the largest rural population (857 million), followed by China (635 million).

- The urban population of the world has grown rapidly since 1950, from 746 million to 3.9 billion in 2014. Asia, despite its lower level of urbanization, is home to 53 per cent of the world's urban population, followed by Europe (14 per cent) and Latin America and the Caribbean (13 per cent).

- Continuing population growth and urbanization are projected to add 2.5 billion people to the world's urban population by 2050, with nearly 90 per cent of the increase concentrated in Asia and Africa.

- Just three countries—India, China and Nigeria—together are expected to account for 37 per cent of the projected growth of the world's urban population between 2014 and 2050. India is projected to add 404 million urban dwellers, China 292 million and Nigeria 212 million.

- Close to half of the world's urban dwellers reside in relatively small settlements of less than 500,000 inhabitants, while only around one in eight live in the 28 mega-cities with more than 10 million inhabitants.

- Tokyo is the world's largest city with an agglomeration of 38 million inhabitants, followed by Delhi with 25 million, Shanghai with 23 million, and Mexico City, Mumbai and São Paulo, each with around 21 million inhabitants. By 2030, the world is projected to have 41 mega-cities with more than 10 million inhabitants. Tokyo is projected to remain the world's largest city in 2030 with 37 million inhabitants, followed closely by Delhi where the population is projected to rise swiftly to 36 million. Several decades ago most of the world's largest urban agglomerations were found in the more developed regions, but today's large cities are concentrated in the global South. The fastest-growing urban agglomerations are medium-sized cities and cities with less than 1 million inhabitants located in Asia and Africa.

- Some cities have experienced population decline in recent years. Most of these are located in the low-fertility countries of Asia and Europe where the overall population is stagnant or declining. Economic contraction and natural disasters have contributed to population losses in some cities as well.

- As the world continues to urbanize, sustainable development challenges will be increasingly concentrated in cities, particularly in the lower-middle-income countries where the pace of urbanization is fastest. Integrated policies to improve the lives of both urban and rural dwellers are needed.

Introduction

In today's increasingly global and interconnected world, over half of the world's population (54 per cent) lives in urban areas although there is still substantial variability in the levels of urbanization across countries (figure 1). The coming decades will bring further profound changes to the size and spatial distribution of the global population. The continuing urbanization and overall growth of the world's population is projected to add 2.5 billion people to the urban population by 2050, with nearly 90 per cent of the increase concen-trated in Asia and Africa. At the same time, the proportion of the world's population liv-ing in urban areas is expected to increase, reaching 66 per cent by 2050.

There is great diversity in the characteristics of the world's urban environs: close to half of urban dwellers reside in relatively small settlements of less than 500,000 inhabitants, while nearly one in eight live in the 28 mega-cities of 10 million inhabitants or more. The number of mega-cities has nearly tripled since 1990; and by 2030, 41 urban agglomerations are projected to house at least 10 million inhabitants each. Whereas several decades ago most of the world's largest urban agglomerations were found in the more developed regions, today's large cities are concentrated in the global South, and the fastest-growing agglomerations are medium-sized cities and cities with 500,000 to 1 million inhabitants located in Asia and Africa.

Figure 1.

Percentage of population residing in urban areas in 2014, selected countries or areas

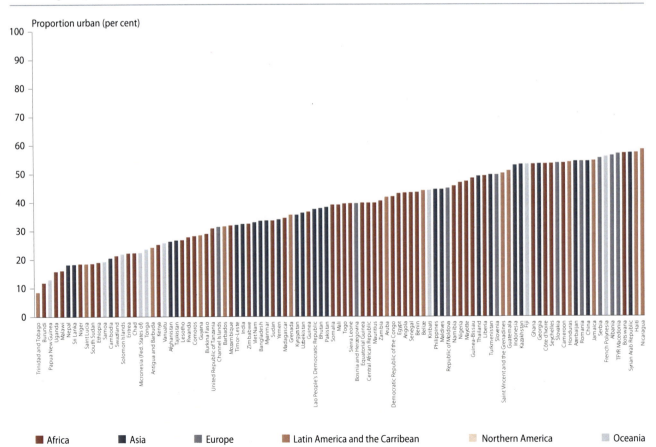

The process of urbanization historically has been associated with other important economic and social transformations, which have brought greater geographic mobility, lower fertility, longer life expectancy and population ageing. Cities are important drivers of development and poverty reduction in both urban and rural areas, as they concentrate much of the national economic activity, government, commerce and transportation, and provide crucial links with rural areas, between cities, and across international borders. Urban living is often associated with higher levels of literacy and education, better health, greater access to social services, and enhanced opportunities for cultural and political participation.

Nevertheless, rapid and unplanned urban growth threatens sustainable development when the necessary infrastructure is not developed or when policies are not implemented to ensure that the benefits of city life are equitably shared. Today, despite the comparative advantage of cities, urban areas are more unequal than rural areas and hundreds of millions of the world's urban poor live in sub-standard conditions. In some cities, unplanned or inadequately managed urban expansion leads to rapid sprawl, pollution, and environmental degradation, together with unsustainable production and consumption patterns.

Urbanization is integrally connected to the three pillars of sustainable development: economic development, social development and environmental protection. The outcome of the Rio+20 United Nations Conference on Sustainable Development, "The future we want" (http://www.un.org/en/sustainablefuture/), recognized both the plight of the urban poor and the need for sustainable cities as matters of great urgency for the United Nations development agenda. Building on that momentum, the third United Nations Conference on Human Settlements (Habitat III), planned for 2016, will bring together world leaders

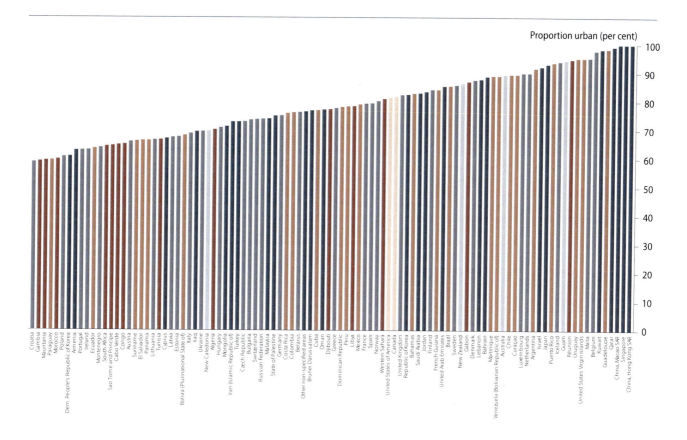

Note: Countries or areas with 90,000 inhabitants or more in 2014.

to review the global urban agenda and to forge a new model of urban development that integrates all facets of sustainable development, to promote equity, welfare and shared prosperity in an urbanizing world.

Accurate, consistent and timely data on global trends in urbanization and city growth are critical for assessing current and future needs with respect to urban growth and for setting policy priorities to promote inclusive and equitable urban and rural development. In order to systematically track levels and trends in urbanization around the world, the Population Division of the Department of Economic and Social Affairs of the United Nations has issued, since 1988, biennial estimates and projections of the urban and rural populations of all countries and of the populations of major urban agglomerations.

This report presents the highlights of the *2014 Revision* of *World Urbanization Prospects*, which contains the latest estimates of the urban and rural populations of 233 countries or areas from 1950 to 2014 and projections to 2050, as well as estimates of population size from 1950 to 2014 and projections to 2030 for all urban agglomerations with 300,000 inhabitants or more in 2014.[1] The annex tables in these Highlights provide data on the estimated and projected urban and rural populations, the percentage of the population that live in urban areas and the annual growth rate of the percentage urban for 233 countries or areas of the world. The tables also show the rank and annual growth rate of urban agglomerations with 5 million inhabitants or more in 2014.

Data and methods

The estimates of the proportion of the population that is urban and the size of urban agglomerations presented in *World Urbanization Prospects: The 2014 Revision* are based on national statistics. Population censuses are the most commonly used sources of data, although estimates obtained from population registers or administrative statistics are also incorporated for some countries.

There is no common global definition of what constitutes an urban settlement. As a result, the urban definition employed by national statistical offices varies widely across countries, and in some cases has changed over time within a country. The criteria for classifying an area as urban may be based on one or a combination of characteristics, such as: a minimum population threshold; population density; proportion employed in non-agricultural sectors; the presence of infrastructure such as paved roads, electricity, piped water or sewers; and the presence of education or health services.

In estimating the proportion urban for *World Urbanization Prospects*, adjustments are made to the national estimates only to ensure consistency of the definitions of urban settlements within countries across time. No attempt is made to impose consistency in definitions across countries. Several efforts are underway at various institutions to produce globally comparable estimates of the urban population with uniform criteria to define urban areas based on satellite imagery of land cover or night-time lights, for example. However, these approaches have not generated, to date, the long historical time series of urbanization estimates required for this report. In interpreting the estimates and projections from *World Urbanization Prospects: The 2014 Revision*, readers should keep in mind the heterogeneity of the urban definition across countries.

---

[1] The full report, descriptions of the data, methodology, and complete data tables representing all countries and areas, regions, income groups, development groups, and periods can be accessed at http://esa.un.org/unpd/wup/index.htm.

In compiling information on city population size, the Population Division has endeavoured to use data or estimates based on the concept of urban agglomeration. When those data are not consistently available, population data that refer to the city as defined by its administrative boundaries were used. However, when the administrative boundaries of cities remain fixed for long periods of time, they are likely to misrepresent the actual growth of a city with respect to both its territory and its population. For a number of cities, the data available refer to two concepts: the city proper as defined by administrative boundaries and its metropolitan area. In those instances, the data referring to the metropolitan area were usually preferred because they are thought to approximate better the territory associated with the urban agglomeration. For any given city, an effort was made to ensure that the time series of population estimates derived from national sources conforms to the same definition over time. Adjustments were made when necessary to achieve internal consistency.

Since censuses are usually taken every 5 or 10 years, to fill the data gaps within the period 1950–2014, the estimates of the proportion urban and the city populations are interpolated or, for the interval between the last data point and 2014, the estimates are extrapolated from the last observed data point. For years beyond 2014, the proportion urban is projected to 2050 and the city populations are projected to 2030. The projection of the proportion urban is based on a projection of the urban-rural growth differential. It is assumed that the urban-rural growth difference for the most recent period available in a given country converges, over a period of 25 years, to a hypothetical urban-rural growth difference, or world norm, that is consistent with historical experience. The method to project city populations is similar, as the last observed city growth rate converges towards an expected value, estimated on the basis of the city population and the growth rate of the overall urban population in the country.

The estimated and projected values of the proportion urban from 1950 to 2050 for each country or area were then applied to the total population as estimated or projected in the medium variant in *World Population Prospects: The 2012 Revision* (United Nations, 2013a) in order to obtain country-level estimates of the urban and rural populations. The *2014 Revision* of *World Urbanization Prospects* updates and supersedes all previous estimates and projections of urban and rural populations and of urban agglomerations published by the United Nations.

"Urbanization in Asia"
UN Photo/Kibae Park

Trends in urbanization

Globally, more people live in urban areas than in rural areas. In 2007, for the first time in history, the global urban population exceeded the global rural population, and the world population has remained predominantly urban thereafter (figure 2). The planet has gone through a process of rapid urbanization over the past six decades. In 1950, more than two-thirds (70 per cent) of people worldwide lived in rural settlements and less than one-third (30 per cent) in urban settlements. In 2014, 54 per cent of the world's population is urban. The urban population is expected to continue to grow, so that by 2050, the world will be one-third rural (34 per cent) and two-thirds urban (66 per cent), roughly the reverse of the global rural-urban population distribution of the mid-twentieth century (also see Annex Table I).

Figure 2.

Urban and rural population of the world, 1950–2050

A majority of the world's population lives in urban areas

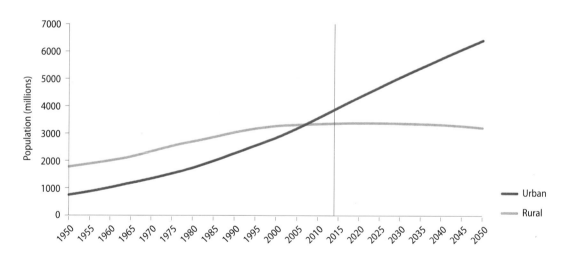

Levels of urbanization vary greatly across regions. In 2014, high levels of urbanization, at or above 80 per cent, characterized Latin America and the Caribbean and Northern America. Europe, with 73 per cent of its population living in urban areas, is expected to be over 80 per cent urban by 2050 (figure 3). Africa and Asia, in contrast, remain mostly rural, with 40 per cent and 48 per cent of their respective populations living in urban areas. Over the coming decades, the level of urbanization is expected to increase in all regions (also referred to as major areas), with Africa and Asia urbanizing faster than the rest. Nevertheless, these two regions, which are projected to reach 56 and 64 per cent urban by mid-century, respectively, are still expected to be less urbanized than other regions of the world.

Urbanization has occurred in all major areas, yet Africa and Asia remain mostly rural

Figure 3.

Urban and rural population as proportion of total population, by major areas, 1950–2050

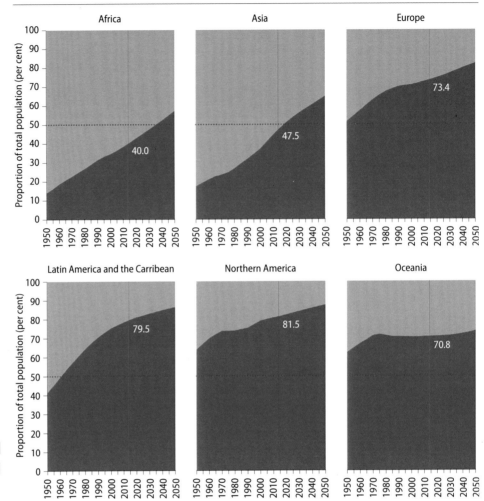

Urban population ▮
Rural population ▯

In 2014, sixteen countries still have low levels of urbanization, i.e. below 20 per cent. The largest among them, with total populations of 10 million inhabitants or more, include Burundi, Ethiopia, Malawi, Niger, South Sudan and Uganda in Africa and Nepal and Sri Lanka in Asia (see Map 1). By 2050, all of these countries are expected to become significantly more urbanized, with as much as twice their respective proportions urban in 2014. In contrast, 59 countries are already more than 80 per cent urban. Among those with populations of at least 10 million inhabitants, the most highly urbanized countries are Belgium (98 per cent urban), Japan (93 per cent), Argentina (92 per cent) and the Netherlands (90 per cent). By 2050, 89 countries are expected to become more than 80 per cent urban. When interpreting the differences in levels of urbanization across countries, it is important to keep in mind the heterogeneity of the urban definition across countries.

Africa and Asia are urbanizing more rapidly than other regions of the world. The rate of urbanization, measured as the average annual rate of change of the percentage urban, is highest in Asia and Africa, where currently the proportion urban is increasing by 1.5 and 1.1 per cent per annum, respectively. Regions that already have relatively high levels of urbanization are urbanizing at a slower pace, at less than 0.4 per cent annually (figure 4). In general, the pace of urbanization tends to slow down as a population becomes more urbanized.

Map 1.

Percentage urban and location of urban agglomerations with at least 500,000 inhabitants, 2014

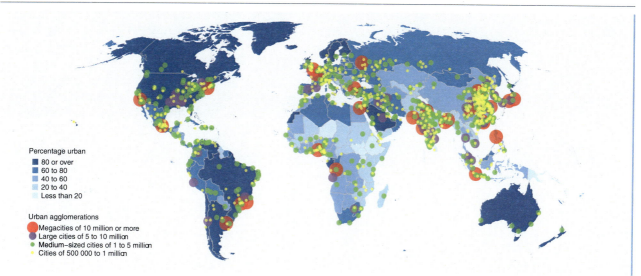

Note: The designations employed and the presentation of material on this map do not imply the expression of any opinion whatsoever on the part of the Secretariat of the United Nations concerning the legal status of any country, territory, city or area or of its authorities, or concerning the delimitation of its frontiers or boundaries.

Figure 4.

Average annual rate of change of the percentage urban by major areas, 1950–2050

The pace of urbanization has varied over time and across major areas

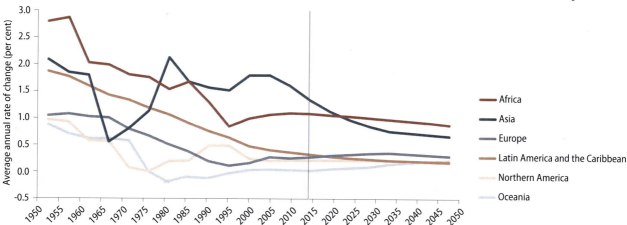

There has been considerable variation across regions in rates of urbanization since 1950. The rate of urbanization in Asia fluctuated widely, mainly as a result of a stagnation of the urbanization process in China in the late 1960s and early 1970s, and its subsequent upturn. Europe, Northern America and Oceania, on the other hand, each experienced a period of stable urbanization, and overall their rate of urbanization has been slow over the last two decades. In Latin America and the Caribbean, the rate of urbanization has declined smoothly over the past six decades. Africa is currently urbanizing faster than in the late 1990s and is expected to be the fastest urbanizing region from 2020 to 2050. Urbanization in developing countries has proceeded faster than in developed countries, but the correlation of the rate of urbanization with economic growth has been weaker than in developed countries (United Nations, 2013b).

While the high-income countries of today have been highly urbanized for several decades, upper-middle-income countries have experienced the fastest pace of urbanization since 1950. In 1950, a majority (57 per cent) of the population in high-income countries already lived in urban areas (figure 5). Their level of urbanization is expected to rise further, from 80 per cent today to 86 per cent in 2050. By contrast, in the upper-middle-income countries of today, only 20 per cent of the population lived in urban areas in 1950, but these countries urbanized rapidly and are now 63 per cent urban. This percentage is expected to rise to 79 per cent urban by 2050. Countries such as Brazil, China, Iran and Mexico are in this group, and have experienced both rapid urbanization and rapid growth of gross national income.

Upper-middle-income countries have experienced the fastest pace of urbanization

High-income countries

Upper-middle-income countries

Lower-middle-income countries

Low income countries

Figure 5.

Proportion urban by income groups, 1950–2050

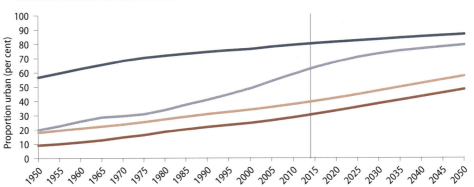

Note: The country classification by income level is based on 2012 GNI per capita from the World Bank and it is kept unchanged throughout the estimates and projections.

In the lower-middle- and low-income countries, the pace of urbanization has been slower until now. Nevertheless, this group of countries is expected to experience faster urbanization than others in the coming decades. In 2014, the proportion of the population living in urban areas was 39 percent in lower-middle-income countries and 30 per cent in low-income countries. By 2050, these countries are expected to reach, on average, 57 and 48 per cent urban, respectively.

The rural population of the world has grown slowly since 1950 and is expected to reach its peak in a few years. Approximately 3.4 billion people currently live in rural areas around the world. That number is expected to remain relatively constant in the coming years. However, sometime after 2020, the world's rural population will start to decline and is expected to reach to 3.2 billion in 2050. This global trend is driven mostly by the dynamics of rural population growth in Africa and Asia, which is home today to nearly 90 per cent of the world's rural population (figure 6a). The rural population of the world resides in a relatively small number of countries. India has the largest rural population (857 million), followed by China (635 million). Together, these two countries account for 45 per cent of the world's rural population. Bangladesh, Indonesia and Pakistan follow, each with over 100 million rural inhabitants. In Africa, the largest rural populations are located in Nigeria (95 million) and Ethiopia (78 million). Between 2014 and 2050, the rural population is expected to increase in about one third of the countries of the world. The largest increases will be registered in Nigeria (50 million), Ethiopia and Uganda (39 and 38 million). The remaining two thirds of countries are expected to have stable or declining rural populations. The largest declines are expected in China, with a decline of 300 million, equivalent to more than one half of their rural population in 2014, and in India, where the number of rural residents is expected to decline by 52 million.

Figure 6a.

A vast majority of the world's rural inhabitants live in Asia, but projected growth is fastest in Africa

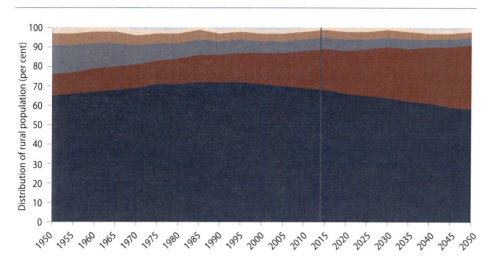

Figure 6b.

Asia will continue to host nearly one half of the world's urban population

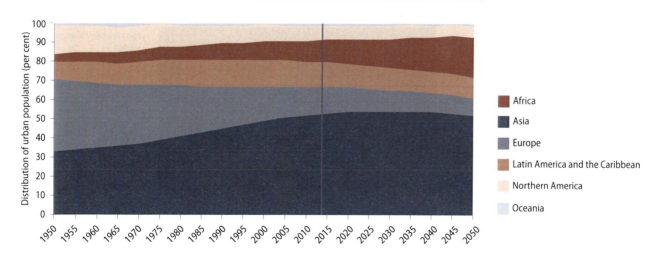

The urban population of the world is expected to increase by more than two thirds by 2050, with nearly 90 per cent of the increase to take place in the urban areas of Africa and Asia. The world's urban population is now close to 3.9 billion and is expected to reach 6.3 billion in 2050. Asia, despite its lower level of urbanization, is today home to 53 per cent of the urban population in the world. Europe has the second highest share of the world's urban population, at 14 per cent, followed by Latin America and the Caribbean with 13 per cent (figure 6b). Over the next four decades, Africa and Asia will experience a marked increase in their urban populations. By mid-century, the urban population of Africa is likely to triple and that of Asia to increase by 61 per cent. As a consequence, close to 90 per cent of the increase in the world's urban population will take place in the urban areas of Africa and Asia. In 2050, most of the urban population of the world will be concentrated in Asia (52 per cent) and Africa (21 per cent).

Figure 9.

The ten largest urban agglomerations in 2014 show varied growth patterns both in the recent past and in future projections

Al-Qahirah (Cairo) ——
New York-Newark ——
Beijing ——
Kinki M.M.A. (Osaka) — ·
Mumbai (Bombay) ····
São Paulo — ·
Ciudad de México (Mexico City) — ·
Shanghai ····
Delhi ——
Tokyo ····

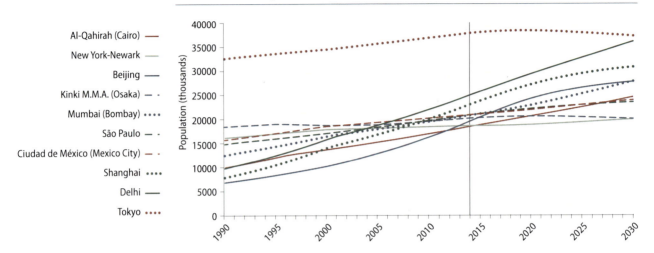

Figure 10.

Population distribution by city size varies across major areas in 2014

Megacities of 10 million or more
Large cities of 5 to 10 million
Medium-sized cities of 1 to 5 million
Cities of 500 000 to 1 million
Urban areas smaller than 500 000

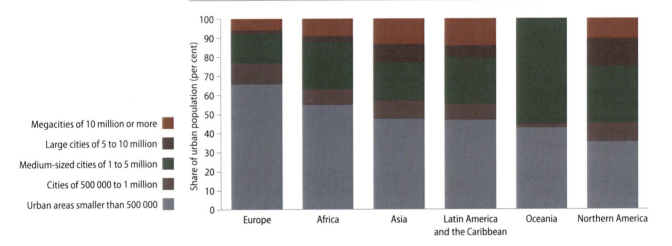

Most megacities and large cities are located in the global South. China alone has six megacities and ten cities with populations between 5 and 10 million in 2014, and it will add one more megacity and six more large cities by 2030. Four of India's cities with 5 to 10 million inhabitants presently are projected to become megacities in the coming years (Ahmadabad, Bangalore, Chennai and Hyderabad), for a total of seven megacities projected in the country by 2030. Outside of China and India, Asia has seven other megacities and eleven other large cities in 2014. Cairo, Kinshasa and Lagos are the only megacities in Africa in 2014, but three more are expected to emerge by 2030, as Dar es Salaam (Tanzania), Johannesburg (South Africa), and Luanda (Angola) are each projected to surpass the 10 million mark. The number of large cities with populations between 5 and 10 million in Africa is also expected to increase, from three in 2014 to twelve in 2030. In Latin America, Bogotá (Colombia) and Lima (Peru) are projected to grow beyond the 10 million mark by 2030, joining the four current megacities of the region: Buenos Aires, Mexico City, Rio de

Janeiro, and São Paulo. Notably, there are varying degrees of uncertainty in the projections of cities, with greater uncertainty for cities like Kinshasa or Luanda where census data have not been collected or reported in decades.

One in five urban dwellers worldwide lives in a medium-sized city with 1 million to 5 million inhabitants. While considered medium-sized by global standards, these cities are, in fact, the largest cities in 79 countries or areas. Examples include Sydney (Australia), Addis Ababa (Ethiopia), and Montevideo (Uruguay). The global population living in medium-sized cities nearly doubled between 1990 and 2014, and is expected to increase by another 36 per cent between 2014 and 2030, growing from 827 million to 1.1 billion. The number of people living in cities of between 500,000 and 1 million inhabitants is expected to grow at a similar pace, increasing from 363 million in 2014 to 509 million in 2030, but continuing to hold only around 10 per cent of the global urban population.

In 2014 close to one half of the world's urban population lives in settlements with fewer than 500,000 inhabitants. While this proportion is projected to shrink over time, by 2030 these small cities and towns will still be home to around 45 per cent of urban dwellers. The proportion of the urban population in small cities varies considerably across regions. Close to two thirds of Europe's urban dwellers reside in small urban places as do more than half of Africa's urban dwellers. In contrast, just one third of urban residents in Northern America live in settlements with fewer than 500,000 people. Regional differences also reflect differences in settlement patterns, as well as variations in the definition of urban areas across countries and regions.

The fastest growing urban agglomerations are medium-sized cities and cities with less than 1 million inhabitants located in Asia and Africa. Between 2000 and 2014 the world's cities with more than 500,000 inhabitants grew at an average annual rate of 2.4 per cent. However, 43 of these cities grew more than twice as fast, with average growth rates in excess of 6 per cent per year (figure 11). Of these, 4 are located in Africa, 38 in Asia (18 in China alone), and 1 in Northern America. By way of comparison, Suzhou, in China's Jiangsu Province, is the only city with more than 5 million inhabitants to have experienced such rapid growth. In general, most of the world's fastest growing urban agglomerations are smaller cities: agglomerations with 500,000 to 1 million inhabitants in 2014 account for 26 of the 43 fastest-growing cities, while another 16 are medium-sized cities with between 1 million and 5 million inhabitants.

Some cities have experienced population decline since 2000, most of which are located in low-fertility countries of Asia and Europe with stagnating or declining populations. A few cities in Japan and the Republic of Korea (for example, Nagasaki and Busan) have experienced population decline between 2000 and 2014. Several cities in the Russian Federation and Ukraine have lost population since 2000 as well. In addition, several capital cities around the world have seen their populations decline between 2000 and 2014, including Bratislava (Slovakia), Riga (Latvia), Sarajevo (Bosnia and Herzegovina) and Yerevan (Armenia). In addition to low fertility, emigration has also contributed to smaller population sizes in some of these cities.

Economic contraction and natural disasters have contributed to population loss in some cities. In the United States, for example, Buffalo and Detroit each experienced net losses of population between 2000 and 2014, concurrent with a loss of industry and jobs in those cities, while New Orleans experienced population decline in the wake of the 2005 Hurricane Katrina.

Figure 11.

The world's fastest growing cities are in Africa and Asia

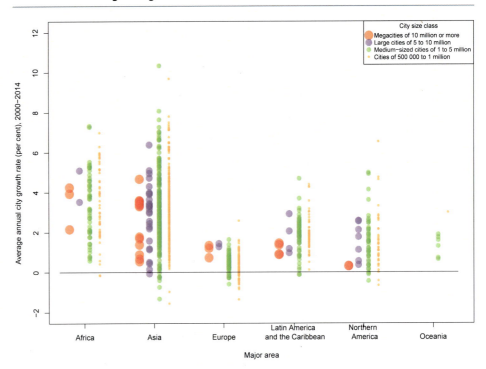

Policy implications

As the world continues to urbanize, sustainable development challenges will be increasingly concentrated in cities, particularly in the lower-middle-income countries where the pace of urbanization is fastest. At the same time, cities offer opportunities to expand access to services, such as health care and education, for large numbers of people in an economically efficient manner. Providing public transportation, as well as housing, electricity, water and sanitation for a densely settled population is typically cheaper and less environmentally damaging than providing a similar level of services to a predominantly rural household. Urban dwellers also have access to larger and more diversified labour markets, and enjoy healthier lives overall.

Governments must implement policies to ensure that the benefits of urban growth are shared equitably and sustainably. The Rio +20 Conference outcome, "The future we want", recognized that cities can lead the way towards economically, socially and environmentally sustainable societies, but that a holistic approach to urban planning and management is needed to improve living standards of urban and rural dwellers alike. Sustainable urbanization requires that cities generate better income and employment opportunities, expand the necessary infrastructure for water and sanitation, energy, transportation, information and communications; ensure equal access to services; reduce the number of people living in slums; and preserve the natural assets within the city and surrounding areas.

Diversified policies to plan for and manage the spatial distribution of the population and internal migration are needed. History has shown that policies that aim to restrict rural-urban migration are ineffective at forestalling city growth, and can even produce economic, social and environmental harms. In recent years, a growing number of countries have been favouring other strategies for rural and urban development, such as allocating land rights, managing land use, land redistribution, creating regional development zones and promoting economic diversification and competitiveness in rural areas through the mobilization of investment and the improvement of rural livelihoods.[2]

Policies aimed at a more balanced distribution of urban growth, avoiding excessive concentration in just one or two very large urban agglomerations within a single country, can also support sustainable development. These policies, as well as those promoting the growth of intermediate-size cities common in Latin America, can help to address the problems of excessive centralization of economic and administrative functions, while also responding to the challenges of providing urban infrastructure and basic social services for the urban poor, and mitigating the negative environmental impacts often associated with large and rapidly growing urban agglomerations.

---

[2] United Nations (2008) *World Population Monitoring, focusing on population distribution, urbanization, internal migration and development.* Report of the Secretary-General to the forty-first session of the Commission on Population and Development, E/CN.9/2008/3

Accurate, consistent and timely data on global trends in urbanization and city growth are critical for assessing current and future needs with respect to urban growth and for setting policy priorities to promote inclusive and equitable urban and rural development. In order to systematically track levels and trends in urbanization around the world and to monitor progress in sustainable development goals in urban and rural areas, Governments, with the support of international cooperation, should continue their efforts to produce more extensive and better quality data on the size, distribution and characteristics of the population.

Successful sustainable urbanization requires competent, responsive and accountable governments charged with the management of cities and urban expansion, as well appropriate use of information and communication technologies (ICTs) for more efficient service delivery. There is a need for building institutional capacities and applying integrated approaches so as to attain urban sustainability.

References

United Nations (1974). *Methods for the Projection of Urban and Rural Population.* Population Studies, No. 55 (United Nations publication, Sales No. E.74.XIII.3).

_____ (1980). *Patterns of Urban and Rural Population Growth.* Population Studies No. 68 (United Nations publication, Sales No. E.79.XIII.9).

_____ (2013a). *World Population Prospects: The Revision 2012.* Volume 1, Comprehensive Tables (United Nations publications ST/ESA/SER.A/336).

_____ (2013b). *World Economic and Social Survey: Sustainable Development Challenges* (E/2013/50/Rev. 1 ST/ESA/344).

UN-Habitat (2012) *State of the World's Cities, 2012/2013.* Nairobi, Kenya. ISBN: 978-92-1-132494-5

"Abidjan, Cote d'Ivoire"
UN/Basile Zoma

Annex

Table I

Urban and rural population, proportion urban and average annual rate of change of the proportion urban

Major area, region, country or area	Population (thousands) Urban 1990	2014	2050	Rural 1990	2014	2050	Proportion urban (per cent) 1990	2014	2050	Average annual rate of change (per cent) 2010–2015
WORLD	2 285 031	3 880 128	6 338 611	3 035 786	3 363 656	3 212 333	43	54	66	0.9
More developed regions[a]	830 952	980 403	1 113 500	317 326	275 828	189 610	72	78	85	0.3
Less developed regions[b]	1 454 079	2 899 725	5 225 111	2 718 460	3 087 828	3 022 723	35	48	63	1.2
Least developed countries[c]	107 335	283 855	895 701	402 019	635 275	914 889	21	31	49	1.7
Less developed regions, excluding least developed countries[d]	1 346 744	2 615 870	4 329 410	2 316 440	2 452 553	2 107 834	37	52	67	1.3
Less developed regions, excluding China	1 126 378	2 115 652	4 148 069	1 854 345	2 446 901	2 684 617	38	46	61	0.9
High-income countries[e]	834 931	1 035 404	1 212 666	287 614	256 311	185 266	74	80	87	0.3
Middle-income countries	1 325 274	2 555 840	4 284 327	2 346 129	2 484 859	2 139 791	36	51	67	1.3
Upper-middle-income countries	793 208	1 541 090	2 155 352	1 153 047	920 812	562 801	41	63	79	1.5
Lower-middle-income countries	532 067	1 014 751	2 128 975	1 193 082	1 564 047	1 576 990	31	39	57	1.1
Low income countries	109 850	268 441	819 856	394 871	616 562	883 673	22	30	48	1.5
Sub-Saharan Africa[f]	132 971	345 617	1 136 822	357 144	579 083	937 624	27	37	55	1.4
AFRICA	196 923	455 345	1 338 566	433 064	682 885	1 054 609	31	40	56	1.1
Eastern Africa	35 564	96 610	378 763	162 822	287 296	490 458	18	25	44	1.7
Burundi	352	1 233	7 025	5 254	9 250	19 666	6	12	26	2.5
Comoros	115	212	576	298	540	932	28	28	38	0.3
Djibouti	448	685	1 028	142	202	216	76	77	83	0.1
Eritrea	517	1 451	6 029	2 755	5 086	8 284	16	22	42	1.9
Ethiopia	6 064	18 363	70 522	41 979	78 143	117 051	13	19	38	2.3
Kenya	3 927	11 476	42 636	19 520	34 070	54 536	17	25	44	1.7
Madagascar	2 721	8 125	30 518	8 825	15 447	24 979	24	34	55	1.9
Malawi	1 092	2 710	12 437	8 355	14 119	28 766	12	16	30	0.9
Mauritius[1]	464	497	570	592	752	661	44	40	46	-0.5
Mayotte	33	108	237	59	120	229	36	47	51	-0.8
Mozambique	3 392	8 454	29 440	10 176	18 019	30 490	25	32	49	0.8
Réunion	496	840	1 089	115	46	36	81	95	97	0.2
Rwanda	391	3 369	13 349	6 824	8 731	12 029	5	28	53	3.7
Seychelles	34	50	65	35	43	35	49	54	65	0.6
Somalia	1 875	4 223	15 664	4 447	6 583	11 412	30	39	58	1.2
South Sudan	765	2 182	8 403	4 999	9 556	16 357	13	19	34	1.0
Uganda	1 942	6 124	33 367	15 593	32 721	70 711	11	16	32	2.1
United Republic of Tanzania[2]	4 813	15 685	68 569	20 672	35 073	60 848	19	31	53	2.3
Zambia	3 091	6 079	25 759	4 753	8 942	18 447	39	40	58	1.1
Zimbabwe	3 033	4 745	11 479	7 429	9 854	14 774	29	33	44	-0.5
Middle Africa	22 566	60 685	192 108	47 434	78 798	124 003	32	44	61	1.2
Angola	2 644	9 580	34 676	7 690	12 558	19 648	26	43	64	1.9
Cameroon	4 787	12 281	34 003	7 284	10 538	14 596	40	54	70	1.1

Major area, region, country or area	Population (thousands)						Proportion urban (per cent)			Average annual rate of change (per cent)
	Urban			Rural						
	1990	2014	2050	1990	2014	2050	1990	2014	2050	2010–2015
Central African Republic	1073	1872	4831	1840	2837	3660	37	40	57	0.6
Chad	1239	2951	12442	4713	10260	21074	21	22	37	0.4
Congo	1295	2961	8168	1089	1597	2409	54	65	77	0.7
Democratic Republic of the Congo	10694	29115	93864	24217	40245	61427	31	42	60	1.2
Equatorial Guinea	130	309	827	244	469	797	35	40	51	0.4
Gabon	655	1487	3004	292	224	298	69	87	91	0.3
Sao Tome and Principe	51	128	293	66	70	95	44	65	75	1.0
Northern Africa	63952	109727	201744	75920	103801	116985	46	51	63	0.4
Algeria	13667	28002	44787	12573	11927	9736	52	70	82	0.9
Egypt	24494	35914	68864	31843	47473	52934	43	43	57	0.1
Libya	3226	4900	7155	1034	1353	1195	76	78	86	0.2
Morocco	11940	19995	31721	12734	13498	11163	48	60	74	0.9
Sudan	5725	13034	38388	14284	25730	38751	29	34	50	0.4
Tunisia	4714	7409	10108	3421	3708	3084	58	67	77	0.3
Western Sahara	187	474	722	30	112	122	86	81	86	0.1
Southern Africa	20539	37238	55422	21514	23653	19140	49	61	74	0.8
Botswana	580	1166	1942	804	873	838	42	57	70	0.4
Lesotho	223	562	1316	1374	1536	1502	14	27	47	2.0
Namibia	391	1073	2538	1024	1275	1205	28	46	68	2.3
South Africa	19146	34168	49103	17647	18972	14303	52	64	77	0.8
Swaziland	198	270	523	665	997	1293	23	21	29	-0.2
Western Africa	54302	151084	510530	125373	189336	304023	30	44	63	1.6
Benin	1725	4612	13574	3277	5987	8563	34	44	61	1.0
Burkina Faso	1217	5056	21299	7594	12364	19633	14	29	52	3.0
Cabo Verde	155	327	493	197	177	143	44	65	78	1.2
Côte d'Ivoire	4767	11126	29997	7349	9679	12342	39	53	71	1.4
Gambia	351	1127	3468	566	782	1398	38	59	71	1.2
Ghana	5331	14118	32192	9298	12324	13477	36	53	70	1.3
Guinea	1687	4418	13764	4333	7626	10702	28	37	56	1.3
Guinea-Bissau	286	848	2268	731	898	1236	28	49	65	1.7
Liberia	1165	2168	6122	937	2229	3270	55	49	65	0.8
Mali	1857	6172	27233	6107	9596	17935	23	39	60	2.1
Mauritania	836	2361	5867	1188	1623	2054	41	59	74	1.1
Niger	1192	3423	24562	6562	15112	44848	15	18	35	1.3
Nigeria	28379	83799	295480	67238	94718	144875	30	47	67	1.9
Saint Helena[3]	2	2	2	3	2	2	43	39	49	-0.0
Senegal	2923	6313	19910	4591	8235	13023	39	43	60	0.7
Sierra Leone	1344	2456	5893	2698	3749	4402	33	40	57	0.9
Togo	1083	2760	8404	2705	4233	6117	29	39	58	1.3
ASIA	1036247	2064211	3313424	2176877	2278044	1850638	32	48	64	1.5
Eastern Asia	467014	960235	1250224	912401	669186	355117	34	59	78	2.0
China[4]	308167	758360	1049948	857262	635424	335029	26	54	76	2.4
China, Hong Kong SAR[5]	5766	7260	8004	28	0	0	100	100	100	0
China, Macao SAR[6]	359	575	797	1	0	0	100	100	100	0
Dem. People's Republic of Korea	11790	15195	19507	8404	9832	7569	58	61	72	0.2
Japan	94546	118136	105784	27703	8864	2546	77	93	98	0.6
Mongolia	1246	2052	3181	938	829	572	57	71	85	1.3
Republic of Korea	31732	40778	44709	11240	8734	6325	74	82	88	0.1
Other non-specified areas	13408	17879	18295	6824	5504	3077	66	76	86	0.6
South-Central Asia[7]	338429	635510	1260028	903305	1201245	1138152	27	35	53	1.2
Central Asia	22347	26372	46417	27740	38901	39737	45	40	54	0.0

Major area, region, country or area	Population (thousands)						Proportion urban (per cent)			Average annual rate of change (per cent)
	Urban			Rural						
	1990	2014	2050	1990	2014	2050	1990	2014	2050	2010–2015
Kazakhstan	9 099	8 850	13 034	7 073	7 757	7 151	56	53	65	-0.2
Kyrgyzstan	1 660	2 002	4 052	2 734	3 623	3 924	38	36	51	0.2
Tajikistan	1 677	2 245	6 185	3 620	6 164	8 907	32	27	41	0.2
Turkmenistan	1 653	2 637	4 303	2 015	2 670	2 266	45	50	66	0.7
Uzbekistan	8 257	10 638	18 842	12 298	18 686	17 488	40	36	52	0.1
Southern Asia	316 082	609 139	1 213 611	875 565	1 162 343	1 098 415	27	34	52	1.2
Afghanistan	2 149	8 221	25 642	9 583	23 059	30 909	18	26	45	1.6
Bangladesh	21 275	53 127	112 443	86 111	105 386	89 504	20	34	56	2.4
Bhutan	88	290	539	448	475	441	16	38	55	2.1
India	221 979	410 204	814 399	646 911	857 198	805 652	26	32	50	1.1
Iran (Islamic Republic of)	31 749	57 170	84 358	24 613	21 301	16 241	56	73	84	0.8
Maldives	56	156	315	160	195	189	26	44	62	2.6
Nepal	1 604	5 130	12 979	16 508	22 991	23 501	9	18	36	2.0
Pakistan	33 967	70 912	155 747	77 124	114 221	115 335	31	38	57	1.1
Sri Lanka	3 216	3 929	7 190	14 108	17 517	16 644	19	18	30	0.0
South-Eastern Asia	140 164	294 409	507 725	303 571	331 573	279 810	32	47	64	1.4
Brunei Darussalam	169	325	458	88	98	88	66	77	84	0.4
Cambodia	1 408	3 161	8 167	7 649	12 247	14 402	16	21	36	0.9
Indonesia	54 634	133 999	227 770	123 999	118 813	93 607	31	53	71	1.5
Lao People's Democratic Republic	655	2 589	6 435	3 589	4 305	4 144	15	38	61	3.1
Malaysia[8]	9 068	22 342	36 163	9 143	7 846	5 950	50	74	86	1.0
Myanmar	10 350	18 023	32 206	31 773	35 696	26 439	25	34	55	1.6
Philippines	30 101	44 531	88 381	31 848	55 566	68 737	49	44	56	-0.4
Singapore	3 016	5 517	7 065	0	0	0	100	100	100	0
Thailand	16 649	33 056	44 335	39 934	34 167	17 406	29	49	72	2.7
Timor-Leste	157	370	1 007	595	782	1 079	21	32	48	2.1
Viet Nam	13 958	30 495	55 739	54 952	62 053	47 958	20	33	54	2.0
Western Asia	90 639	174 057	295 447	57 600	76 040	77 558	61	70	79	0.5
Armenia	2 390	1 874	1 961	1 155	1 110	821	67	63	70	-0.3
Azerbaijan[9]	3 879	5 172	7 136	3 338	4 343	3 356	54	54	68	0.5
Bahrain	437	1 192	1 684	59	152	151	88	89	92	0.1
Cyprus	512	773	977	255	380	379	67	67	72	-0.2
Georgia[10]	3 005	2 311	2 350	2 455	2 011	1 212	55	53	66	0.3
Iraq	12 211	24 116	55 653	5 307	10 653	15 683	70	69	78	0.1
Israel	4 065	7 202	11 189	434	620	655	90	92	94	0.1
Jordan	2 461	6 263	10 283	897	1 242	1 228	73	83	89	0.3
Kuwait	2 018	3 421	6 268	42	58	74	98	98	99	0.0
Lebanon	2 247	4 354	4 874	456	612	442	83	88	92	0.1
State of Palestine[11]	1 409	3 328	7 408	672	1 108	1 499	68	75	83	0.3
Oman	1 197	3 030	4 380	614	896	685	66	77	86	0.6
Qatar	442	2 249	2 978	34	19	6	93	99	100	0.1
Saudi Arabia	12 411	24 355	35 839	3 795	5 015	4 549	77	83	89	0.3
Syrian Arab Republic	6 093	12 588	26 245	6 359	9 398	10 461	49	57	72	0.7
Turkey	31 966	55 279	79 189	22 028	20 559	15 418	59	73	84	0.7
United Arab Emirates	1 428	8 054	14 058	378	1 392	1 421	79	85	91	0.4
Yemen	2 468	8 496	22 976	9 322	16 472	19 520	21	34	54	1.7
EUROPE	505 991	545 382	581 113	217 257	197 431	127 954	70	73	82	0.3
Eastern Europe	211 281	203 201	191 714	99 482	90 134	54 809	68	69	78	0.1
Belarus	6 770	7 100	6 274	3 490	2 208	1 086	66	76	85	0.5
Bulgaria	5 855	5 277	4 205	2 966	1 891	872	66	74	83	0.5
Czech Republic	7 767	7 843	8 900	2 559	2 898	2 318	75	73	79	-0.1
Hungary	6 837	7 030	7 327	3 548	2 903	1 628	66	71	82	0.7

Major area, region, country or area	Population (thousands) Urban 1990	2014	2050	Rural 1990	2014	2050	Proportion urban (per cent) 1990	2014	2050	Average annual rate of change (per cent) 2010–2015
Poland	23 374	23 149	23 854	14 775	15 071	10 225	61	61	70	-0.1
Republic of Moldova[12]	2 041	1 555	1 463	2 323	1 906	1 021	47	45	59	0.0
Romania	12 438	11 771	11 903	10 934	9 869	5 906	53	54	67	0.3
Russian Federation	108 732	105 318	98 040	39 417	37 149	22 856	73	74	81	0.1
Slovakia	2 981	2 932	3 161	2 296	2 522	1 829	56	54	63	-0.4
Ukraine	34 486	31 226	26 588	17 173	13 715	7 070	67	69	79	0.3
Northern Europe	70 985	81 747	101 259	21 128	19 191	14 509	77	81	87	0.3
Channel Islands[13]	44	51	73	97	112	106	31	31	41	0.3
Denmark	4 361	4 935	5 847	779	705	514	85	88	92	0.2
Estonia	1 115	868	815	450	416	306	71	68	73	-0.2
Faroe Islands	15	21	28	33	29	25	31	42	53	0.5
Finland[14]	3 958	4 577	5 071	1 029	866	622	79	84	89	0.2
Iceland	231	313	399	24	20	16	91	94	96	0.1
Ireland	2 009	2 944	4 474	1 522	1 733	1 520	57	63	75	0.4
Isle of Man	36	45	60	34	41	39	52	52	61	0.1
Latvia	1 845	1 376	1 252	819	665	422	69	67	75	-0.1
Lithuania	2 499	2 001	1 910	1 199	1 007	647	68	67	75	-0.1
Norway[15]	3 051	4 084	5 717	1 189	1 008	838	72	80	87	0.3
Sweden	7 113	8 251	10 782	1 446	1 381	1 152	83	86	90	0.2
United Kingdom	44 708	52 280	64 830	12 507	11 209	8 301	78	82	89	0.3
Southern Europe	92 660	108 935	119 969	50 727	47 068	30 920	65	70	80	0.3
Albania	1 256	1 797	2 345	2 191	1 389	749	36	56	76	1.9
Andorra	52	69	79	3	12	16	95	86	83	-0.6
Bosnia and Herzegovina	1 777	1 515	1 839	2 750	2 310	1 492	39	40	55	0.3
Croatia	2 590	2 506	2 606	2 203	1 766	1 000	54	59	72	0.5
Gibraltar	27	29	27	0	0	0	100	100	100	0
Greece	7 261	8 644	9 158	2 899	2 484	1 510	71	78	86	0.4
Holy See[16]	1	1	1	0	0	0	100	100	100	0
Italy	37 922	42 029	46 640	18 910	19 041	13 375	67	69	78	0.2
Malta	339	410	405	36	20	12	90	95	97	0.2
Montenegro	295	397	403	319	225	154	48	64	72	0.3
Portugal	4 743	6 675	7 564	5 156	3 936	2 279	48	63	77	0.9
San Marino	22	30	32	2	2	1	90	94	96	0.0
Serbia[17]	4 906	5 251	4 738	4 829	4 218	2 336	50	55	67	0.1
Slovenia	1 010	1 031	1 225	994	1 044	798	50	50	61	-0.2
Spain[18]	29 299	37 349	41 601	9 584	9 717	6 624	75	79	86	0.3
TFYR Macedonia[19]	1 161	1 202	1 306	848	906	575	58	57	69	0.0
Western Europe	131 064	151 499	168 171	45 921	41 038	27 716	74	79	86	0.3
Austria	5 044	5 621	6 984	2 626	2 906	2 370	66	66	75	0.0
Belgium	9 617	10 901	11 891	362	243	164	96	98	99	0.0
France	42 098	51 253	63 174	14 748	13 388	10 037	74	79	86	0.3
Germany	58 851	62 067	60 220	21 636	20 585	12 346	73	75	83	0.3
Liechtenstein	5	5	9	24	32	36	17	14	20	-0.2
Luxembourg	309	482	666	73	54	40	81	90	94	0.4
Monaco	29	38	53	0	0	0	100	100	100	0
Netherlands	10 227	15 107	16 304	4 663	1 695	615	69	90	96	0.8
Switzerland	4 884	6 024	8 870	1 790	2 134	2 107	73	74	81	0.1
LATIN AMERICA AND THE CARIBBEAN	313 876	495 857	673 631	131 327	127 565	107 935	71	80	86	0.3
Caribbean	19 851	29 897	38 440	14 411	12 916	9 207	58	70	81	0.8
Anguilla	8	14	15	0	0	0	100	100	100	0
Antigua and Barbuda	22	22	30	40	69	85	35	24	26	-2.0
Aruba	31	43	49	31	60	54	50	42	47	-0.7

Major area, region, country or area	Population (thousands)						Proportion urban (per cent)			Average annual rate of change (per cent)
	Urban			Rural						
	1990	2014	2050	1990	2014	2050	1990	2014	2050	2010–2015
Bahamas	205	317	430	52	66	64	80	83	87	0.1
Barbados	85	90	122	175	196	192	33	32	39	-0.4
British Virgin Islands	6	13	20	10	15	15	38	46	58	0.7
Cayman Islands	25	59	67	0	0	0	100	100	100	0
Cuba	7 777	8 666	7 833	2 824	2 593	1 559	73	77	83	0.1
Dominica	45	50	59	26	22	17	63	69	78	0.4
Dominican Republic	4 001	8 219	12 003	3 244	2 310	1 318	55	78	90	1.4
Grenada	32	38	42	64	68	53	33	36	44	-0.1
Guadeloupe[20]	371	461	487	14	7	6	96	98	99	0.0
Haiti	2 027	6 009	10 936	5 083	4 453	3 417	29	57	76	2.4
Jamaica	1 169	1 527	1 900	1 196	1 272	908	49	55	68	0.4
Martinique	309	360	365	49	45	35	86	89	91	-0.0
Montserrat	1	0	1	9	5	5	13	9	13	-0.3
Sint Maarten (Dutch part)	29	46	61	0	0	0	100	100	100	0
Caribbean Netherlands	10	15	19	3	5	5	78	75	80	0.0
Curaçao	124	145	162	22	17	17	85	89	91	-0.1
Puerto Rico	3 270	3 449	3 424	248	234	187	93	94	95	-0.0
Saint Kitts and Nevis	14	18	29	27	37	39	35	32	43	0.2
Saint Lucia	41	34	52	98	150	155	29	18	25	0.1
Saint Vincent and the Grenadines	45	55	69	63	54	42	41	50	62	0.7
Trinidad and Tobago	104	115	123	1 118	1 229	1 032	9	9	11	-1.5
Turks and Caicos Islands	9	31	42	3	3	2	74	92	96	0.4
United States Virgin Islands	91	102	100	13	5	3	88	95	97	0.2
Central America	74 880	124 682	187 158	40 226	44 995	41 675	65	73	82	0.4
Belize	89	150	301	99	190	289	47	44	51	-0.4
Costa Rica	1 539	3 749	5 482	1 539	1 189	707	50	76	89	1.4
El Salvador	2 631	4 230	5 425	2 713	2 154	1 487	49	66	78	0.7
Guatemala	3 655	8 107	21 157	5 235	7 753	10 269	41	51	67	0.9
Honduras	1 984	4 472	9 497	2 920	3 789	3 987	40	54	70	1.1
Mexico	61 475	97 766	134 828	24 602	26 034	21 274	71	79	86	0.4
Nicaragua	2 166	3 607	6 006	1 972	2 563	2 349	52	58	72	0.5
Panama	1 340	2 603	4 462	1 146	1 323	1 313	54	66	77	0.4
South America	219 145	341 279	448 033	76 690	69 653	57 052	74	83	89	0.3
Argentina	28 378	38 293	48 339	4 247	3 510	2 684	87	92	95	0.2
Bolivia (Plurinational State of)	3 776	7 388	13 193	3 018	3 460	3 428	56	68	79	0.6
Brazil	110 623	172 604	210 238	39 025	29 429	20 882	74	85	91	0.3
Chile	11 003	15 881	19 403	2 211	1 892	1 437	83	89	93	0.2
Colombia	22 741	37 265	53 083	10 566	11 665	9 859	68	76	84	0.4
Ecuador	5 577	10 152	17 184	4 547	5 831	5 877	55	64	75	0.3
Falkland Islands (Malvinas)	1	2	3	1	1	0	74	76	85	0.7
French Guiana	87	215	443	30	41	52	75	84	89	0.4
Guyana	214	229	314	511	575	501	30	28	39	0.2
Paraguay	2 069	4 110	7 471	2 180	2 807	2 975	49	59	72	0.4
Peru	15 001	24 088	35 405	6 771	6 681	5 679	69	78	86	0.4
Suriname	267	359	445	139	184	176	66	66	72	-0.1
Uruguay	2 767	3 253	3 549	343	166	92	89	95	97	0.2
Venezuela (Bolivarian Republic of)	16 638	27 439	38 964	3 103	3 412	3 412	84	89	92	0.0
NORTHERN AMERICA	212 935	291 860	390 070	69 351	66 376	56 130	75	81	87	0.2
Bermuda	60	65	64	0	0	0	100	100	100	0
Canada	21 181	29 006	39 616	6 477	6 519	5 611	77	82	88	0.2
Greenland	44	49	46	11	8	4	80	86	92	0.5
Saint Pierre and Miquelon	6	5	6	1	1	0	89	90	93	0.1
United States of America	191 645	262 734	350 338	62 862	59 849	50 515	75	81	87	0.2

Major area, region, country or area	Population (thousands)						Proportion urban (per cent)			Average annual rate of change (per cent)
	Urban			Rural						
	1990	2014	2050	1990	2014	2050	1990	2014	2050	2010–2015
OCEANIA	19 059	27 473	41 807	7 911	11 356	15 067	71	71	74	0.0
Australia/New Zealand	17 480	25 025	36 533	3 015	3 157	2 980	85	89	92	0.1
Australia[21]	14 601	21 099	31 346	2 496	2 531	2 389	85	89	93	0.2
New Zealand	2 880	3 926	5 187	518	626	591	85	86	90	0.0
Melanesia	1 097	1 817	4 398	4 416	7 637	11 460	20	19	28	0.2
Fiji	303	473	597	425	414	322	42	53	65	0.7
New Caledonia	100	181	293	68	79	72	60	70	80	0.9
Papua New Guinea	623	971	2 976	3 534	6 505	10 116	15	13	23	-0.0
Solomon Islands	43	125	355	269	448	655	14	22	35	2.2
Vanuatu	27	67	177	119	192	295	19	26	38	1.2
Micronesia	258	343	481	155	171	190	62	67	72	0.2
Guam	118	158	218	12	9	8	91	94	96	0.1
Kiribati	25	46	85	46	58	71	35	44	55	0.2
Marshall Islands	31	38	54	17	15	13	65	72	80	0.4
Micronesia (Fed. States of)	25	23	39	71	81	91	26	22	30	0.1
Nauru	9	10	11	0	0	0	100	100	100	0
Northern Mariana Islands	39	49	47	5	6	5	90	89	91	-0.1
Palau	11	18	26	5	3	2	70	86	93	0.9
Polynesia[22]	224	289	395	324	391	437	41	42	47	-0.2
American Samoa	38	48	55	9	7	7	81	87	89	-0.1
Cook Islands	10	15	20	7	5	4	58	74	82	0.3
French Polynesia	115	157	209	84	123	128	58	56	62	-0.2
Niue	1	1	1	2	1	0	31	42	59	1.9
Samoa	35	37	57	128	155	185	21	19	23	-1.0
Tokelau	0	0	0	2	1	1	0	0	0	0
Tonga	22	25	45	74	81	95	23	24	32	0.3
Tuvalu	4	6	9	5	4	3	41	59	75	1.7
Wallis and Futuna Islands	0	0	0	14	13	13	0	0	0	0

Notes

a   More developed regions comprise Europe, Northern America, Australia/New Zealand and Japan.

b   Less developed regions comprise all regions of Africa, Asia (excluding Japan), Latin America and the Caribbean plus Melanesia, Micronesia and Polynesia.

c   The least developed countries are 49 countries, 34 in Africa, 9 in Asia, 5 in Oceania plus one in Latin America and the Caribbean.

d   Other less developed countries comprise the less developed regions excluding the least developed countries.

e   The country classification by income level is based on 2012 GNI per capita from the World Bank.

f   Sub-Saharan Africa refers to all of Africa except Northern Africa.

1   Including Agalega, Rodrigues, and Saint Brandon.

2   Including Zanzibar.

3   Including Ascension, and Tristan da Cunha.

4   For statistical purposes, the data for China do not include Hong Kong and Macao, Special Administrative Regions (SAR) of China.

5   As of 1 July 1997, Hong Kong became a Special Administrative Region (SAR) of China.

6   As of 20 December 1999, Macao became a Special Administrative Region (SAR) of China.

7   The regions Southern Asia and Central Asia are combined into South-Central Asia.

8   Including Sabah and Sarawak.

9   Including Nagorno-Karabakh.

10   Including Abkhazia and South Ossetia.

11   Including East Jerusalem.

12   Including Transnistria.

13   Refers to Guernsey, and Jersey.

14   Including Åland Islands.

15   Including Svalbard and Jan Mayen Islands.

16   Refers to the Vatican City State.

17   Including Kosovo.

18   Including Canary Islands, Ceuta and Melilla.

19   The former Yugoslav Republic of Macedonia.

20   Including Saint-Barthélemy and Saint-Martin (French part).

21   Including Christmas Island, Cocos Keeling Islands, and Norfolk Island.

22   Including Pitcairn.

Table II

Population size and ranking of urban agglomerations with more than 5 million inhabitants as of 1 July 2014

Urban Agglomeration	Country or area	Population (thousands)			Rank			Average annual rate of change (per cent)
		1990	2014	2030	1990	2014	2030	2010–2015
Tokyo	Japan	32 530	37 833	37 190	1	1	1	0.6
Delhi	India	9 726	24 953	36 060	12	2	2	3.2
Shanghai	China	7 823	22 991	30 751	20	3	3	3.4
Ciudad de México (Mexico City)	Mexico	15 642	20 843	23 865	4	4	10	0.8
São Paulo	Brazil	14 776	20 831	23 444	5	5	11	1.4
Mumbai (Bombay)	India	12 436	20 741	27 797	6	6	4	1.6
Kinki M.M.A. (Osaka)	Japan	18 389	20 123	19 976	2	7	13	0.8
Beijing	China	6 788	19 520	27 706	23	8	5	4.6
New York-Newark	United States of America	16 086	18 591	19 885	3	9	14	0.2
Al-Qahirah (Cairo)	Egypt	9 892	18 419	24 502	11	10	8	2.1
Dhaka	Bangladesh	6 621	16 982	27 374	24	11	6	3.6
Karachi	Pakistan	7 147	16 126	24 838	22	12	7	3.3
Buenos Aires	Argentina	10 513	15 024	16 956	10	13	18	1.3
Kolkata (Calcutta)	India	10 890	14 766	19 092	7	14	15	0.8
Istanbul	Turkey	6 552	13 954	16 694	25	15	20	2.2
Chongqing	China	4 011	12 916	17 380	43	16	17	3.4
Rio de Janeiro	Brazil	9 697	12 825	14 174	13	17	23	0.8
Manila	Philippines	7 973	12 764	16 756	19	18	19	1.7
Lagos	Nigeria	4 764	12 614	24 239	33	19	9	3.9
Los Angeles-Long Beach-Santa Ana	United States of America	10 883	12 308	13 257	8	20	26	0.2
Moskva (Moscow)	Russian Federation	8 987	12 063	12 200	15	21	31	1.2
Guangzhou, Guangdong	China	3 072	11 843	17 574	63	22	16	5.2
Kinshasa	Democratic Republic of the Congo	3 683	11 116	19 996	50	23	12	4.2
Tianjin	China	4 558	10 860	14 655	37	24	22	3.4
Paris	France	9 330	10 764	11 803	14	25	33	0.7
Shenzhen	China	875	10 680	12 673	308	26	29	1.0
London	United Kingdom	8 054	10 189	11 467	18	27	36	1.2
Jakarta	Indonesia	8 175	10 176	13 812	17	28	25	1.4
Seoul	Republic of Korea	10 518	9 775	9 960	9	29	43	-0.0
Lima	Peru	5 837	9 722	12 221	28	30	30	2.0
Bangalore	India	4 036	9 718	14 762	42	31	21	4.0
Chennai (Madras)	India	5 338	9 620	13 921	30	32	24	3.0
Bogotá	Colombia	4 740	9 558	11 915	34	33	32	2.7
Chukyo M.M.A. (Nagoya)	Japan	8 407	9 373	9 304	16	34	49	0.5
Johannesburg	South Africa	3 709	9 176	11 573	48	35	34	3.2
Krung Thep (Bangkok)	Thailand	5 888	9 098	11 528	27	36	35	2.4
Chicago	United States of America	7 374	8 739	9 493	21	37	46	0.3
Hyderabad	India	4 193	8 670	12 774	39	38	28	3.3
Lahore	Pakistan	3 970	8 500	13 033	44	39	27	3.1
Tehran	Iran (Islamic Republic of)	6 365	8 353	9 990	26	40	42	0.9
Wuhan	China	3 417	7 838	9 442	57	41	47	1.0
Dongguan	China	553	7 410	8 701	516	42	51	0.9
Chengdu	China	2 955	7 289	10 104	71	43	41	3.8
Hong Kong	China, Hong Kong SAR	5 766	7 260	7 885	29	44	61	0.7
Nanjing, Jiangsu	China	2 893	7 127	9 754	74	45	44	3.6
Ahmadabad	India	3 255	7 116	10 527	59	46	38	3.4
Thành Pho Ho Chí Minh (Ho Chi Minh City)	Viet Nam	3 038	7 100	10 200	67	47	40	3.3
Foshan	China	1 008	6 989	8 353	267	48	53	1.1
Kuala Lumpur	Malaysia	2 098	6 629	9 423	109	49	48	3.3

Urban Agglomeration	Country or area	Population (thousands)			Rank			Average annual rate of change (per cent)
		1990	2014	2030	1990	2014	2030	2010–2015
Baghdad	Iraq	4 092	6 483	9 710	41	50	45	2.4
Santiago	Chile	4 616	6 472	7 122	36	51	64	0.7
Ar-Riyadh (Riyadh)	Saudi Arabia	2 325	6 195	7 940	92	52	58	4.0
Shenyang	China	3 651	6 194	7 911	51	53	59	2.1
Madrid	Spain	4 414	6 133	6 707	38	54	70	1.4
Hangzhou	China	1 476	6 121	8 822	163	55	50	4.6
Toronto	Canada	3 807	5 901	6 957	46	56	65	1.7
Xi'an, Shaanxi	China	2 157	5 867	7 904	102	57	60	3.2
Miami	United States of America	3 969	5 771	6 554	45	58	74	1.1
Belo Horizonte	Brazil	3 548	5 667	6 439	53	59	75	1.1
Dallas-Fort Worth	United States of America	3 219	5 603	6 683	60	60	71	2.0
Pune (Poona)	India	2 430	5 574	8 091	86	61	57	2.9
Philadelphia	United States of America	4 725	5 571	6 158	35	62	78	0.5
Kitakyushu-Fukuoka M.M.A.	Japan	5 269	5 528	5 355	31	63	95	-0.2
Singapore	Singapore	3 016	5 517	6 578	69	64	73	2.0
Houston	United States of America	2 922	5 516	6 729	72	65	68	2.5
Surat	India	1 468	5 398	8 616	166	66	52	4.8
Haerbin	China	2 392	5 351	6 860	87	67	67	2.2
Luanda	Angola	1 390	5 288	10 429	175	68	39	4.0
Barcelona	Spain	4 101	5 207	5 685	40	69	89	1.3
Suzhou, Jiangsu	China	1 067	5 156	8 098	249	70	56	6.3
Atlanta	United States of America	2 184	5 032	6 140	101	71	79	2.5